ARISE

AWAKE | RESIST | INCREASE | SHINE | ELEVATE

J.P. BURNETT

WESTBOW
PRESS®
A DIVISION OF THOMAS NELSON
& ZONDERVAN

WestBow Press books may be ordered through
booksellers or by contacting:

WestBow Press
A Division of Thomas Nelson & Zondervan
1663 Liberty Drive
Bloomington, IN 47403
www.westbowpress.com
844-714-3454

ISBN: 978-1-6642-4084-1 (sc)
ISBN: 978-1-6642-4085-8 (hc)
ISBN: 978-1-6642-4083-4 (e)

Library of Congress Control Number: 2021914382

Print information available on the last page.

WestBow Press rev. date: 08/17/2021

CONTENTS

PREFACE

This book is for those like me who have been functioning for a long time but seem stuck in different aspects of our lives. *ARISE* seeks to encourage and help us awaken our relationship with God. This will empower us to revive our dreams and prophetic words spoken over us so we can fulfill our role in God's master plan. After you've read *ARISE*, I want you to take action and regain sight of what God sees in you.

You see, sometimes we are guilty of being stagnant in life, especially as it pertains to our spiritual lives; we can be comfortable, lazy, or fearful. Ouch! Let me talk about me for a bit before we start to go deeper and journey through this book together. My story is that I have grown up in church since the age of three. I went through Sunday school, Youth Department, and Men's Ministry. I have also served in a series of ministries and positions in the local church and on a national level in my denomination.

Yes, this is the part where I say that it has not always been smooth, because I have sinned, focused on other things, and not given God the full attention that He deserves. Here's the thing: I have also gone through deep church hurt that caused me to lose my hair, I have had to deal with death in my family and even financial difficulties where I lost US$50,000 on a house down payment. I mention these because you may have gone through circumstances like these or other situations with similar or even worse results. It is these circumstances as well as other challenges that would test one's ability to **A**wake, **R**esist, **I**ncrease, **S**hine, and **E**levate.

INTRODUCTION

At this book's core it is truly an encouragement for every believer, especially for those who may feel stuck in their Christian walk or other areas of their life: relationships, parenting, or navigating various spheres of influence in your career or physical health. This theme or call to action was birthed before the 2020 pandemic but has become even more real and will be applicable for seasons to come.

At first this acronym started from my 2020 New Year's message, "In spite of … You are still here … He has kept you; you have purpose to fulfill → A.R.I.S.E." If you are reading this book, you are still here! Despite a pandemic and one of the most difficult times the world has gone through in recent history, God has kept you because you are chosen for this time, this season, and you have a purpose to fulfil. Yes, *you*. You were born with a purpose; don't entertain the enemy's lies that you do not have a purpose.

We have all been given gifts and talents to be used for the glory and honor of God and the advancement of His kingdom. Jesus was the promised Messiah, and He came and played His role and continues to do so today. God has called you to be great, whether it is worship leader, encourager, creative, student, scientist, prophet, mentor, intercessor, administrator, entrepreneur, evangelist, pastor, parent, child, teacher, apostle, social activist, or sanitation engineer.

Why has it been difficult to *ARISE* and fulfill purpose? It is because the enemy knows your worth. The devil wants to destroy us all. His mission, as stated in John 10:10 (emphasis added): "The thief cometh not, but for to *steal,* and to *kill,* and to *destroy.*" He understands that the more he does to distract you, the less the kingdom of God is advanced.

Let me plug in here that I believe that "busyness" is from the enemy, the more we are consumed with adding things to do, we tend to put our attention on our earthly to-do list than our kingdom to-do list. It is important for us to balance and not add roles or responsibilities that are not in line with our purpose. It is okay to say *no.* (Note to self: Come on, J.P., read that sentence again.) In addition, we are often very tired, which affects our devotional life and ability to fulfill purpose; sounds familiar, doesn't it? As I stated before, we are all born with a purpose, and I want us to look at a very familiar story and see some of the teaching points.

> After the wise men were gone, an angel of the Lord appeared to Joseph in a dream. "Get up! Flee to Egypt with the child and his mother," the

angel said. "Stay there until I tell you to return, because Herod is going to search for the child to kill him." That night Joseph left for Egypt with the child and Mary, his mother. (Matthew 2:13–14 NLT)

God always speaks to us in different ways: directly (Holy Spirit), dreams, visions, and people to give us direction and warnings to prevent us from failing. He promised to provide a way of escape. It is critical that we do not hesitate when God speaks. You have to know when the season is over and God is calling you to new things, places, or ministries. At times we stay too long in places because we get comfortable or wonder why at this age we need to move and change. There are times when we will be afraid because of what we are hearing or seeing. God could have given Joseph the full instructions in the first instance, but it can be in these times that He teaches us to trust Him and grow our faith. It is important that we are obedient "in spite of."

For the rest of this year and beyond don't allow the enemy to frustrate you; believe God's will. *As long as we do not ARISE the enemy is happy,* but you have to **Awake, Resist, Increase, Shine, and Elevate.**

1

JUST A CONVERSATION

MANY OF YOU READING THIS BOOK MAY BE OVERWHELMED OR want things to change. You want to be better and even be the best in every facet of your life. I know about feeling this way, and you may know people who are feeling this way. There are persons going through unexplained sicknesses, loss, parents with cancer, financial challenges, school challenges, family challenges, and work challenges. I know we unpacked a lot there, and you may be reminded or thinking about what you and your friends or family are going through or have gone through. The year 2020 brought a pandemic, which compounded any other challenges we were facing.

I had to deal with going online for church. PS: I don't really like to be in front of cameras. I owned a taxi that got completely wrecked, I had a leaking roof, and there was a death in my family. The past year has been filled with a lot of _____. You fill in the blank because I am sure we all have different words to describe it.

It is in these times we can begin to just survive

and forget the promises of God for our lives. I want to remind us that as long as we are alive there is hope because God's promises are yes and amen. Be reminded of Romans 5:3–5, which says, "And not only so, but we glory in tribulations also: knowing that tribulation worketh patience; and patience, experience; and experience, hope: and hope maketh not ashamed; because the love of God is shed abroad in our hearts by the Holy Ghost which is given unto us."

Remember that when you go through challenges or trials, they teach you and help you to grow and know that God still loves you and is still for you.

Stop for a moment and breathe. I am here to remind you today that the first thing we need to do is stop. I need you to stop, take a deep breath, and be reminded that it is God who gives us life. The breath you have taken is a reminder that there is so much more that you can still do. *It's a reminder that Christ empowers us to do everything.* We are more than overcomers.

Don't get caught up in the motions. There are times when we are overwhelmed or the enemy puts up smoke screens. I believe the adversary creates distractions to keep us from spending time with God and focusing on His will and other things that matter. You see, there are times for some of us, if not all of us, when we get caught up in all that is happening with and around us. We have grown accustomed to the routine; we go to church, go to work, cook, or do this or the other. Sometimes when it comes to God, He gets less of our attention, and that's even when we are fulfilling our duties but not necessarily doing them out of love.

We must seek His kingdom first and make time for family. We can't just keep reading or hearing about God but not doing. We have to exercise and practice our gifts. He has also called some to start businesses and be influencers in different spheres of life. His kingdom is advanced and grown when we walk in purpose. What we do for God will last.

We need to *push* for and take time for what is

important. God is important and then our family and friends. To paraphrase from Francis Chan, God then family, but there is supposed to be a large space for Him because He is in a dimension all on His own. Some of us need to come back to that place where we don't do things just to keep up the motions or because of emotions but out of devotion to God.

Speak life over your situations and dreams. It is not over! Be reminded about the faithfulness of God. As the scripture says, He will not abandon us forever, even if it feels that way at times.

Second Peter 1:3 declares, "According as His divine power hath given unto us all things that pertain unto life and godliness, through the knowledge of him that hath called us to glory and virtue." We have been given access to everything related to life and godliness. As you continue to read this book, I hope that it gives you a call to action and that you know that you can thrive in all aspects of your life. I pray this puts things into perspective so that you can *ARISE*. I truly believe that we are living in a time that God wants His people to *ARISE*.

As we move on to *ARISE*, the first thing we must do is *AWAKE*.

2

AWAKE

ARISE [9]

WHEN WE HEAR THE WORD AWAKE, WE IMMEDIATELY THINK of someone who was sleeping. Romans 13:11 (AMP) informs us, "Do this, knowing that this is a critical time. It is already the hour for you to awaken from your sleep [of spiritual complacency]; for our salvation is nearer to us now than when we first believed [in Christ]." We are living in a time where we must awake from the sleeping areas in our lives and here are two reasons why. First, in order to be all that God wants us to be, we have to shake up ourselves and begin to do what we are called to do.

I know. I know! Typing or saying "I will do it" is easier than actually doing it. It is important that when we meet our Maker, He can tell us, "Well done, my good and faithful servant." We must not be guilty of not doing the things He asked or prompted us to do. Let's look at one of the biblical accounts that reminds us not only how we must awaken but also how timing is critical.

In the account of Joseph mentioned in the introduction, Joseph was wakened from a dream.

There are times when we wake up for ourselves and other moments when an external force alerts and awakens us. In this story, God is the one who wakes up Joseph and tells him what is about to happen. It was extremely important that Joseph acted upon God's instructions right away. Let me put a plug here and say that timely obedience is key. There are occasions when if we miss the timing, we can miss out on what God has in store for us. The Bible calls these *kairos* moments, and when we don't move with the wind of God, we miss the momentum to be propelled into our destiny. In this account, if Joseph hadn't left right away, Jesus could have been killed, as Herod had decided to execute all boys two years and under.

Before we continue, let's look at the dictionary definition of "awake," taken from Merriam-Webster Online.

> *Awake* (adjective): fully conscious, alert, and aware; not asleep.

After looking at the definition, I would like to point out that it is possible to operate in a sleepy state with certain facets of our lives, which can prevent us from being fully alert and aware.

The second reason you must be awake is that there are people who are waiting for you to operate in fullness because you are destined to impact their lives. Yes, there are people waiting on *you*! Let me help you here, the majority of people don't like to *awake* unless they have to. In the next chapter, I will share a bit on how most of us view ourselves, but let me remind you now of how God sees you. How He sees you will give you reasons to *awake*.

How I Am Seen by God

HIS CHILD

For all who are led by the Spirit of God are children of God. So you have not received a spirit that makes you fearful slaves. Instead, you received God's Spirit when he adopted you as his own children. Now we call him, "Abba, Father." (Romans 8:14–15 NLT)

He came to his own people, and even they rejected him. But to all who believed him and accepted him, he gave the right to become children of God. (John 1:11–12 NLT)

See how very much our Father loves us, for he calls us His children, and that is what we are! (1 John 3:1 NLT)

These scriptures clearly state that you and I are children of God. With this come rights and privileges. Be reminded of who you are and whose you are. Your heavenly Father cares about you and loves you. Sometimes it is a case of tough love because every good parent knows how to get the best out of their children, and they are always there to help and guide along the way. Even when we make mistakes, our heavenly Father is still there to help us become all that we *need* to be, not necessarily want. Take note. If God takes care of the birds and good earthly fathers know how to give good gifts, so much more your heavenly Father gives good things to those who ask Him.

CONQUEROR

> Yet in all these things we are more than conquerors and gain an overwhelming victory through Him who loved us [so much that He died for us]. (Romans 8:37 AMP)

Through God we have access to victory. He knows who we are and knows we have the ability to conquer any situation we face with His help. Jesus is the conquering Lion of the tribe of Judah, the captain of the hosts of heaven's armies. When God looks at us, He sees us seated in heavenly places in Christ Jesus. When God looks at you, He sees the mark of an overcomer, and what may appear to be defeat to you at times is just a setup for your next victory. *Do not lose sight of what He sees.*

DESIGNER'S ORIGINAL

> So God created human beings in His
> own image. In the image of God He
> created them; male and female He
> created them …. Then God looked
> over all He had made, and He saw
> that it was very good! (Genesis 1:27,
> 31 NLT)

Scientists all over the world still marvel and cannot fully unravel the depth and intricacies that make up the human body. Each person is hardwired with their very unique fingerprint, retina scan, and DNA; even your vocal patterns are unique to you. God spoke the world into existence, but He took the time to create man in His image and likeness. None of the other created beings have the privilege of communing with God the way we do. You are special. Even parents of identical twins can distinguish between their children; how much more your heavenly Father who is acquainted with every detail, down to the number of hairs on your head.

This is how God, the King of kings and your heavenly Father, sees you: designer's original, conqueror and child. You have reasons to *awake* and reflect on how God sees you. It is time to *awake* and come forth from the dormant areas of your life. Lazarus was brought back to life after four days, which some surely thought was impossible. I want to emphasize here that with God all things are possible. So resurrect the dead, inactive, sleeping, or sluggish parts of your life.

I've had to *awake* twice within recent times. As a Christian I had to make an honest assessment that I was just getting by or doing the basics in some aspects of my life for years. As the impact of the pandemic became evident, I had to adjust and go deeper with God by spending more time in His presence. I'll talk about the other time in the next chapter. Was I sleeping? Maybe not, but I was keeping my eyes closed so I did not have to open my eyes to see what I needed to do. So I encourage you to open your eyes and *awake* from the sleeping or stagnant places in your life. This includes prayer, reading your Bible, developing your heavenly language, reading books for edification, and exerting your energies and gifts in ministry (especially the one God called you to), family, marriage, work, and business.

CALL TO ACTION – Ask the Holy Spirit to help you assess where you are. Visualize the way God sees you, where He wants you to be, and what He wants you to do. Write down those areas where you need to *awake* and ask God for strategy.

_____

_____

_____

_____

_____

_____

_____

_____

_____

_____

3

RESIST

WHAT DOES IT MEAN TO RESIST?

Resist: **1** to exert oneself so as to counteract or defeat

2 to withstand the force or effect of

A S YOU AND I HAVE WRITTEN DOWN THE AREAS WHERE WE need to *awake* and have sought God for godly strategy, there are certain things we need to *resist*. The main three categories that I consider are self, others, and the enemy.

The other things we must resist that are a subset of the main three are concerns, worries, anxieties, and fear. Most times we don't fulfill purpose, dreams or *increase* because of challenges with these. The truth is even though we are reminded of how God sees us, you and I know that we doubt from time to time or even forget. I have been guilty of this as well, so we must first *resist* self.

Let's take some time and reflect on the physical and figurative mirror. As you read and contemplate the following questions, pause and take all the time you need to respond to them. You can consider writing or recording your responses.

Are you contented with yourself or where you are?

What is your self-esteem like?

We can see ourselves as lower than we really are or at times think more highly of ourselves than we should because we may be found looking through a skewed lens, where we only see our faults or overestimate our good qualities. *Resist* doubt whenever it pops into your mind. The Bible has examples of persons who doubted themselves at various periods. We have an example in Exodus chapter 4 (NLT). Verse 1 says, "But Moses protested again, 'What if they won't believe me or listen to me?'" Verse 10 reiterates, "But Moses pleaded with the Lord, 'O Lord, I'm not very good with words. I never have been, and I'm not now, even though you have spoken to me. I get tongue-tied, and my words get tangled.'" Let's not focus more on our faults but understand the power of God to use *you*. Here's a reminder from 2 Corinthians 12:9 (NLT):

"Each time he said, 'My grace is all you need. My power works best in weakness.' So now I am glad to boast about my weaknesses, so that the power of Christ can work through me."

We must *resist* others (naysayers). Some of us don't *increase* because we think about what others say about us. As humans, we want everyone to be happy with our decisions or at least happy for us. However (and it's never good when someone says *however* or *but*), there are people who criticize and even try to block you from doing all that God wants you to do and become. Unfortunately, there are times when it's family or people who are close to you.

Imagine after all Moses's self-doubt and deciding to still go, that it was his brother and sister who spoke against and questioned his leadership. Numbers 12:1–2 (NLT) says, "While they were at Hazeroth, Miriam and Aaron criticized Moses because he had married a Cushite woman. They said, 'Has the Lord spoken only through Moses? Hasn't he spoken through us, too?' But the Lord heard them." Other times it can be people who just don't like having you in their group or doing as well as they do because the ministry or success must only have a certain type. In Luke 9:49–50 (NLT), "John said to Jesus, 'Master, we saw someone using your name to cast out demons, but we told him to stop because he isn't in our group.' 50 But Jesus said, 'Don't stop him! Anyone who is not against you is for you.'"

People tend to want to classify others. They can do this based on your title, career, role in church, race, financial standing, or educational level; they may even consider your sense of fashion. Based on that, some may see you as too proud or timid, maybe too reserved. Some may think you are not good enough. Persons may look at your position and think you should be better. Think about the essential workers. How many nurses, farmers, truck drivers, trash collectors, and sanitation personnel were viewed as menial before 2020, and how are they viewed now? They are now being heralded and honored globally.

We must also *resist* the enemy. There are two scriptures that give us advice for this.

> Therefore, put on the complete armor of God, so that you will be able to [successfully] resist *and* stand your ground in the evil day [of danger], and having done everything [that the crisis demands], to stand firm [in your place, fully prepared, immovable, victorious]. (Ephesians 6:13 AMP)

It is critical that we daily put on the armor of God. Think about a soldier going to war without any weapons or shields. They can be severely wounded or even taken out on the frontline. We must have our armor on so that when the devil tries to come at us, we can *resist* him.

We must also submit to God as in James 4:7 (AMP): "So submit to [the authority of] God. Resist the devil [stand firm against him] and he will flee from you." You see, once we are under

God's covering and not thinking we can do it on our own, the devil has to flee.

THE ENEMY — WHO IS STILL TRYING TO DEVOUR YOU!

The enemy would try to cause problems with work, ministry, family, and finances. As I stated before, this is the time he would try to put doubt in your mind about what is going on and about whether God is concerned. Let me remind you that, beyond any shadow of a doubt, God is still in control.

Soundness of mind or a well-balanced mind is critical so that you do not make any rash decisions or entertain wrong thoughts. The adversary will try to distract you, but put on the helmet of salvation, and let your thoughts be Christ-centered. Let me put it this way. It is important to remember that the adversary would try to hinder you because of who you are destined to be. Don't think that he stopped because he is practicing social distancing. Two points are noteworthy: the word of God tells us that He doesn't give us anything more than we can handle. Also just as in the case of Jesus after He was tempted by the devil, the same enemy left Him for a season, and angels ministered to Him. God always makes provisions for us to be ministered to; He restores us in due season.

For those of you who are thinking about launching your business, *resist* doubt, and silence the voice of the adversary who may be trying to dissuade you. To the parent who is trying to adjust with the rapidly changing educational environment or just trying to provide for your family, *resist* the enemy who may try to keep you bound in cycles of poverty and the naysayers who suggest you should just accept your lot in life.

One of the key strategies for resisting the enemy is knowing we are stronger together. Now if ever there was a time when we should be continually encouraging each other, so the adversary cannot single out anyone, especially the injured or those now starting their journey, it's now. Ecclesiastes 4:12 (NLT) says, "A person standing alone can be attacked and defeated, but two can stand back-to-back and conquer. Three are even better, for a triple-braided cord is not easily broken."

Reflect on the example of David:

- For forty days Goliath kept taunting Israel, and nobody was standing up against him. David chose to stand up; he'd had enough. He was reminded of who he was serving. The truth is, sometimes we forget. There were more skilled people than him. The enemy will always tell you that you cannot handle it.
- David was young. *Resist* when you hear you are too young or (like Caleb) too old from any of the three above (self, others, enemy). There will be people who would tell you that you are not ready; "Who do you think you are?"
- Saul wanted David to wear his armor, but it was too heavy. Sometimes we try to use others' methods, but what is needed for the situation is your own God-given tactics. You should not try to fit in someone else's armor;

what was designed to protect others may hinder your movement and agility.

- David's slingshot showed God's power. Some may view his instrument inadequate for taking down a giant, but it showed the power of God to use a simple weapon for victory. Sometimes the choice of weapon or strategy that may seem obvious or recommended isn't the one that God wants us to use. We have to follow His strategy in order to obtain the victory. Second Corinthians 10:4 (AMP) says, "The weapons of our warfare are not physical [weapons of flesh and blood]. Our weapons are divinely powerful for the destruction of fortresses." The battle is the Lord's!

- We need to make sure the job is completed. Too many times we stop when we think our opponent is down. When resisting, we must push until the job or battle is completed. Note that David cut off Goliath's head even though he was down. Some might think this is overkill, but I believe that, as Christians, when we think we are gaining ground, we tend to slow down rather than advancing full throttle and finishing the job. Ever played a game where the person losing comes back to win? Don't be the one snatching defeat from the jaws of victory; press on until the win is secure.

You can't resist on shaky ground. Let's look at 1 Peter 5:7–9 (AMP); I would just highlight verse 9 but please take a moment and read the entire excerpt. Verse 9 (emphasis added) says, "But *resist* him, be firm in your faith [against his attack—rooted, established, immovable], knowing that the same experiences of suffering are being experienced by your brothers and sisters throughout the world. [You do not suffer alone.]" Picture having to plant your feet on shaky ground or someplace where you can't manage secure footing; it becomes easier for someone to push you over. When resisting, we must do so from a firm foundation. Put on the armor of God, and stand firm in your place.

Whether we like to admit it or not, sometimes things happen in our lives that cause us to doubt and can even lead us to being depressed. Think back about Elijah and one of the most fascinating recorded miracles and victories of that era. When his life was threatened, he began to doubt and became dejected. In that account, even in his time of depression and wanting to die, the Lord sent an angel to minister to him.

I recently experienced a loss when a relative that I lived with died, it was very hard and still is challenging. I had to *arise*, more so *resist*, because these are the times where we can doubt or question or become disheartened. When we go through any type of difficult situation, we tend to add compound interest. Basically, we look at everything that is wrong in our lives. We must *resist* the urge to do this because it can lead to depression. So resist doubt, resist fear, resist anxiety. Let me remind you and me of this verse: "He who began a good work is faithful to complete it."

CALL TO ACTION – List the areas where you need to *resist*. Write or record aspects of self that you need to *resist*: inhibitions, fears, and negative habits or cycles. Set boundaries for persons who are hindering you from fulfilling your dreams. Write daily biblical affirmations to silence the accusations of the enemy.

_____

_____

_____

_____

_____

_____

_____

_____

4
INCREASE

WHEN I THINK ABOUT INCREASING, LET ME BE HONEST: THE first two things that come to my mind are increasing in finances and bulking up muscles. What is the first thing that comes to your mind when you think about increase?

In this chapter we want to focus on increasing in all areas, but let's look at your faith first. Now you may ask, why faith first? But faith is the foundation for trusting God and for launching out into different spheres. I am looking at faith as defined in Hebrews 11:1, the type of faith that is "the substance of things hoped for, the evidence of things not yet seen."

You see, faith is the basis where we can step out and be and do all that God wants us to. This includes domains like business, creative abilities, career, family, and ministry. We all want to *arise* and be the best versions of entrepreneurs, mentors, workers, spouses, parents, and siblings that we can be. As I mentioned in the previous chapter, we must *resist* fear; and I believe that as faith increases, fear dwindles. I believe that many times we continue to ask ourselves, "What if?" rather than stepping out and seeing "What could?" If you're anything like me, sometimes you tend to have faith but without the works. So how do we increase our faith, so that the next time an opportunity presents itself, we are ready to launch?

Let's start with the simple song that most persons would be acquainted with, "Read Your Bible and Pray Every Day." Reading the Bible gives us confidence, because it reminds us of all the things God did with ordinary people just like you and me. In Hebrews 11 we are reminded of many other persons who because of their faith went on to do much more than anyone expected. Praying also builds our faith because as we make our petitions and we receive answers to our appeals, we increase in faith. It also helps us as we can hear from God who gives us direction in order to fulfill purpose.

When the enemy tries to sow seeds of doubt, weed them out, and sow faith. Like the father of the child in scripture who cried out, "Lord, I believe; help my unbelief!" we can cry out to God to remove our disbelief. Faith comes by hearing the *word*. At times we begin to question God's plan, but His thoughts and ways are higher than ours. Remind yourself of what God has done for you or your family, like the Psalmist who said, "I recall all you have done, O Lord; I remember your wonderful deeds of long ago. They are constantly in my thoughts. I cannot stop thinking about your mighty works" (Psalm 77:11–12 NLT). Ask God to reveal Himself to you just as with doubting Thomas.

Faith is not a feeling but a choice. Faith is a foundation, and it should not be easily swayed. When earthquakes and hurricanes come, it will stand. Think about the story of the three little pigs. Straw blows away quickly; sticks take a little more time but eventually fall; but bricks (Solid Rock) stand the test. The house may be shaken, but it stays secure. Your faith may be shaken at times but once entrenched in the *word* of God it will stay grounded.

If any of you lacks wisdom, you should ask God, who gives generously to all without finding fault, and it will be given to you. But when you ask, you must believe and not doubt, because the one who doubts is like a wave of the sea, blown and tossed by the wind. That person should not expect to receive anything from the Lord. Such a person is double-minded and unstable in all they do. (James 1:5–8 NIV)

Another area where we all need to *increase* is wisdom and knowledge. We can do this by reading books and watching videos that are in relation to where God is calling us and what He wants us to do. This can apply to your business, work, ministry, and education. The truth is that I never liked to read. Ironic, isn't it? Now I am writing a book for others to read. But I have realized more and more that as a young pastor and even as an entrepreneur, it is critical to get information about the areas we are in and where we wish to go. Think about it with me: most people, if not all, would have at least done some studies or some type of training for the job that they are in. As we continue to change globally in all sectors of life, it has become even more important to increase in knowledge, keep up with what is happening and also what is trending, and be innovative.

Another way we must *increase* is in surrendering all facets of our lives to Christ. At times we hold back from giving Him rule and reign in our lives. It is here that John tells us in John 3:30, "He must increase, but I must decrease." How do we let Him *increase*? We can do so by denying ourselves, relinquishing our rights to determine our destiny, and allowing God to lead and direct our choices.

Think about the athletes who train and push themselves to increase in speed, muscle, reflexes, etc. We must realize that we need to be equipped properly when we are in different seasons. For example, it would be quite challenging to use anything other than sneakers for exercising. We must use appropriate strategies to deal with and overcome any challenges and be where God has predestined. Let me put it another way: if we don't continue to train or increase, we can expect to be defeated by the enemy.

Consistency and discipline are domains where most of us can put up our hands and acknowledge that at times we lack in these traits. Generally speaking, people tend to want to do the bare minimum but expect great results. Ouch! Even though we may have had the greatest strategies and plans, sometimes things fall through when we are not consistent with the execution. For example, we can be inclined to pray a few times and stop when we begin to see breakthrough, rather than persisting until completion. First Corinthians 9:24–27 (NLT) says,

> Don't you realize that in a race everyone runs, but only one person gets the prize? So run to win! All athletes are disciplined in their training. They do it to win a prize that will fade away, but we do it for an eternal prize. So I

run with purpose in every step. I am not just shadowboxing. I discipline my body like an athlete, training it to do what it should.

I also want us to consider that we must *increase* in the fruit of the Spirit. As we *increase* our engagement with the Holy Spirit, we are better equipped to face life and fulfill purpose. This helps you to be able to deal with daily challenges. The Holy Spirit produces this kind of fruit in our lives: love, joy, peace, patience, kindness, goodness, faithfulness, gentleness, and self-control. You draw on different aspects more than others depending on the season of life you are in. Let's delve some more into a couple of these.

We must increase in patience (yes, J.P., patience!). Isaiah 60:22 (NLT) says, "At the right time, I, the Lord, will make it happen." It is His timing that is perfect, not ours! Trust me, I know this sounds easy on paper. Let's think about an example of a door, the kind that opens only after you hear a click. First, we must read the instructions or listen to the guard or employee who tells us what to do. Sometimes we don't read the instructions of God's *word* or listen to a minister or the Holy Spirit but still expect the door to open when we pull on it. The other thing we do is sometimes push or pull too slow or too fast and get frustrated. You see, waiting for the right timing is important—you have to wait for the *click*!

Sometimes God is telling us to do something that could change or propel our business, relationships, family or ministry to the next dimension, but we move too slow and miss the timing. The other struggle is when we receive a personal prophetic word but we rush it, which has the same effect: we're unable to enter the door. So learn to wait; as the *word* says, "They that wait upon the Lord shall renew their strength; they shall mount up with wings as eagles" (Isaiah 40:31).

Let's continue to use some analogies and see where we can *increase*. We are going to look at *increase* in humility. Most of us like to do things for ourselves or want God to do things directly for us and not use third parties.

I am reminded of the story I read of a man who was drowning and God sent a boat, a whale, and a helicopter, but each time help came, the man said He was waiting on God. Eventually he drowned. Upon reaching heaven, he asked God, "How come you did not save me?"

God replied, "I sent help." Don't let your mind-set or pride prevent you from receiving the help that God has sent to support and deliver you.

We must recognize when we need help but also *accept it*. I know you probably just took a deep breath there. Going back to the analogy of the door with the click opening, every now and again we have loads in our hands when trying to open a door, and we cannot get out or in without help. Your help can be someone on the inside of the door, the security guard, or just another person. They can help you open the door. For the believer, God sits on the inside of the door of your heart and has angels that stand as security ready to make an open way. To reiterate, you need to know when you require help or encouragement from someone else.

Closely following humility is the aspect of *increase* in good, godly friends. You also need persons in your life who will enhance you; iron sharpens iron. "As iron sharpens iron, so a friend sharpens a friend" (Proverbs 27:17 NLT). I know a lot of people like to say, "It's only me and Jesus!" or "I am keeping to myself," or "I don't need any help." I know that some of you may have adopted this philosophy because of past experiences with others. I want to *shout* this point; Jesus sent the disciples in twos and that iron sharpens iron. You need to *increase* in great supportive friends. Having said that, please understand that *some of the persons who come into your life are for seasons.* Don't carry people who are not supposed to be in certain seasons. It is like wearing summer clothes in the middle of winter; "That ain't right!" I truly believe as a family and community of God, we are stronger together. We have wrongfully adopted the approach of not sharing struggles or genuinely supporting each other because of real or perceived shame or fear of rejection. Confessing your faults one to another is critical as we help one another. The adversary tries to keep us bound through shame, but friends, brothers, sisters, please don't wait till you are drowning to ask for help. Even with tangible needs, reach out, call a prayer partner, and seek counsel from godly people in the area you are trying to *increase.*

CALL TO ACTION – Write down or record a voice note about the areas where you need to *increase*. Find the necessary resources such as videos, books, and people that can help enhance and propel you to your next level. Six months from today review your recording, and evaluate your development.

_____

_____

_____

_____

_____

_____

_____

_____

5

SHINE

YOU ARE THE LIGHT OF THE WORLD. A TOWN BUILT ON A HILL cannot be hidden. Neither do people light a lamp and put it under a bowl. Instead they put it on its stand, and it gives light to everyone in the house. In the same way, let your light shine before others, that they may see your good deeds and glorify your Father in heaven. (Matthew 5:14–16 NIV)

Let me allow you ten (10) seconds to rehash the first line of that scripture. *You* are the light of the world. When we take time to ponder it, being the light of the world may seem weighty or impossible because of where we currently are. I know for some of us, we started off very bright, but as time and situations have passed, we have become dim. The other thing we must be careful about—and I am sure you have heard this repeatedly—is that we must stay connected to the source and ensure our light does not get dim. This is where I encourage you to come back in alignment with the *Son*, who gives us energy. Jesus is the one who empowers us to *shine* as brightly as we can in all aspects of our life.

We were reminded in an earlier chapter of how God sees us. Once we are a true reflection of that image, we should always be shining. Think of how the moon reflects the sun, it does not generate its own light, but based on its position it reflects the sunlight. In our case we must always reflect the *Son*. Note that if we are not in the right position, then we cannot truly display His glorious light. This is why we must *resist* sin and *increase* in holiness; we must decrease, and He must increase. We must *increase* in wisdom and knowledge for where God has called and is calling us, so we can *shine*.

My previous pastor always reminded us that we don't get a second chance to make a first impression. Let that sink in for a moment. When you meet and interact with people or when others see you as a worker, businessperson, parent, or minister, do they see you as bright or dim? You may ask what I mean by "dim" in these scenarios. If someone were to observe you in the workplace signing in to work earlier than your actual arrival time, or if as a businessperson you are known as someone who is always scheming or giving bad service, then your light is dim. If as a parent you take zero interest in how your child views God or you refuse to have patience with your children when they make simple mistakes, you can be viewed as dim. If someone categorizes you as a minister (we all have some form of ministry) who values acquiring money more than the kingdom, you are dim. You may also be labeled as a wolf in sheep's clothing. I always believed that the way we live and operate is our greatest testimony and the best way that we can evangelize people. Most of us may not be Bible tract distributors or be able to go on the mission field, so it is vital that our lifestyles reflect Christ.

The *key* is to *shine* as brightly as God wants you to. This may sound weird to some but certain rooms or settings require a different wattage. There are times where you have to be a 100-watt bulb or a 75-watt or 60-watt bulb; just check with the Chief Architect or Designer (God) to know what is best suited. There are times we are not shining or lighting up the room with the wattage that is required. If a bulb was designed for a certain wattage and it does not get enough electricity, it will not shine as bright as it should. This is why we must be properly connected to receive all the power that is required to reach our full potential, especially in these times. We must be humble enough to recognize that we are *lit* because of God. In our humility we can radiate the most, as God's power works best in weakness.

We all have varying personalities and different motives for shining our light. There are persons who can shine but prefer to stay in the background; and then we have persons who love to shine and display themselves in everything. If you prefer a background role but the Lord is calling you to the frontline, I understand that you may have inhibitions, fears, and even anxiety about stepping into the light. These reservations may seem real to you, but you must remind yourself of the truth of God's word and allow that to shape your reality. We should not be upset or hide when God is causing us to *shine*. If you are not operating in the wattage you are called for, know that some sectors of society are not being illuminated; some lives are not being "lit up." Let me say that again: certain people and sectors are waiting on *you* to step up and *shine*.

On the flip side, others want to *shine* all the time. Pride can step in depending on the motives and cause a fall. It is critical that you radiate the right intensity of light where God wants you to. We should never push ourselves into the spotlight when God has not orchestrated it. I have struggled with this occasionally—always wanting to be the hero and trying to shine my light in places where God did not call or send me. I learned that God doesn't always have to use me, and it is not about me or my abilities, but it is about Him.

For those of us who are always concerned about the opinions of others or pleasing people; it is important to note that when your light is shining brightly it has the possibility of being a glare to others. The enemy or envious people never like it when you are shining too brightly. Similar to when you've just *awakened*, it would take some time for your eyes to adjust to the light. Know that the enemy will try to get you to lower your light's intensity, especially if it is blinding his eyes. The scripture tells us the devil is like a roaring lion, and lions hunt mainly in the dark to be undetected. Consider as well thieves who prefer to break in during the night to avoid detection. When you are consumed by things not working out, it can overshadow you or surround you with darkness. The enemy uses this as an opportune time to pounce. Your adversaries usually don't attack in well-illuminated places.

So maintain your *shine* so you can spot the enemy; you are the light of the world. Again, your adversary understands that if you are a great example of a businessperson, mentor, spouse, parent, minster, etc., then you will *shine*. You will show the world that Jesus is causing you to be great. That is why the adversary throws things at you so that you will be dim.

The scripture in Isaiah 60:1–2 (TLB) states:

> Arise, my people! Let your light shine for all the nations to see! For the glory of the Lord is streaming from you. Darkness as black as night shall cover all the peoples of the earth, but the glory of the Lord will shine from you.

Another version says it this way:

> Arise [from spiritual depression to a new life], shine [be radiant with the glory *and* brilliance of the Lord]; for your light has come, and the glory *and* brilliance of the Lord has risen upon you. For in fact, darkness will cover the earth and deep darkness *will cover* the peoples; But the Lord will rise upon you and His glory *and* brilliance will be seen on you. (AMP)

The Lord tells us to *ARISE*, and what is notable here is that darkness will cover the earth. It seems we are in dark times, but the glory of the Lord and His brilliance will be seen on you. You can be going through the most difficult situations and still have a smile on your face. When you display the joy of the Lord through tough times; that causes your light to *shine* to others. When the favor of God hits you or you spend time in the presence of God, just as with Moses your face will definitely *shine*. Excelling as a student despite limited resources and maintaining humility in the midst of it makes you *shine*. Taking the time to train your children and bring out their inherent uniqueness puts God's glory on display. You see, in whichever area we want to *shine*, we must seek God for strategies; as it is not by might or power but by insight from the Holy Spirit.

> The night is far spent, the day is at hand: let us therefore cast off the works of darkness, and let us put on the armour of light. (Romans 13:12)

Now that we have explored shining in all areas, I want to close this section by saying that it is important that we don't just concentrate on the secular arena of our lives but we also focus our *shine* on kingdom business. Matthew 6:33 should be our mantra; we are to seek the kingdom of God first. If we want to see the church and the kingdom of God grow, we cannot only expect others to work. You have been called! Even if you think you are just a minuscule part of the body, you are still a vital part. Each part of the body plays a role.

We can no longer say that we are unable to do the things God is requiring of us. Paul shared the secret of living in every situation and concludes that, in every circumstance, we can do all things through Christ who strengthens us (see Philippians 4:13). We have to ask forgiveness for the times we told God, "Not me; I cannot do it." Think about Peter, who was empowered to speak on the day of Pentecost. He might not have done what he did if he had not been filled by the Holy Spirit.

The truth is, if God is calling you to do

something, he knows *you can do it!* God used Moses, though he gave God several reasons why he could not be the one to lead the Israelites. Once he surrendered, God caused him to *shine*—literally! Don't you know that the same power that raised Christ from the dead resides in you? Second Timothy 1:7 (NLT) says, "For God has not given us a spirit of fear and timidity, but of power, love, and self-discipline." So push past your fears, your insecurities and inhibitions, your unbelief at times, and position yourself for the light of the Son to *shine* through you.

CALL TO ACTION – Visualize where God wants you to be and what He wants you to do. Take the lists from *Awake, Resist,* and *Increase,* and create a vision board that captures the spheres where God wants you to SHINE. You should also include a summary of things you need to avoid on your journey.

_____

_____

_____

_____

_____

_____

_____

_____

6

ELEVATE

BUT THE GOD OF ALL GRACE, WHO HATH CALLED US UNTO HIS eternal glory by Christ Jesus, after that ye have suffered a while, make you perfect, stablish, strengthen, settle you. (1 Peter 5:10)

God promises to establish us but it is not always an easy process. After you have suffered, and you have learned from all your experiences, this is when God settles you on a firm foundation. You can only be elevated if your foundation is firm. Imagine a skyscraper; it can only be built to last if its foundation is secure. Contemplating elevation can be exciting when we think about acquiring or achieving more or moving higher. Keep in mind that in order to elevate, we also have to stretch, which as I alluded to can be uncomfortable. Some persons prefer to stay where they are because they are contented, but being open to the stretching process is well worth it.

When we hear the word *elevate* as Christians, some if not most become cautiously excited or happy. This usually happens because we believe that the higher we go, the harder the battles or trials will be. I am sure you would be expecting me to fully dispel that claim right now. Sorry to disappoint, but let me put it in a way that should change the way that you see it. Apostle Nigel Lewis stated that "we must change our perspective about facing more difficult demons and think that the more you elevate you are putting other demons out of business because you have overcome them."

The word *elevate* can be defined as:

1: to lift up or make higher: RAISE

2: to raise in rank or status – was elevated to chairman

3: to improve morally, intellectually, or culturally

As you *elevate*, some people may not see it right away, but in due season, God will cause your light to *shine* as He establishes you. Think about an escalator or an elevator. There are two key things to note. First, sometimes the ride takes a while, but you still get to where you need to go—to the top.

Second, you have to know when and how to get on and off of an escalator; you have to time it just right. Similarly, you must know when it is time to jump on board with God elevating you and come off at the level He is calling you to. Sometimes when you are elevated, persons who are already at that level may wonder if you are on the correct floor, as they have not seen you there before or may not know that you have been elevated. That's okay; in due time they will know that God has authorized and orchestrated your being there.

THINGS TO CONTEMPLATE IN THE ELEVATION PROCESS

Be Humble

> So humble yourselves under the mighty power of God, and at the right time he will lift you up in honor. (1 Peter 5:6 NLT)

In order for the Lord to raise you up, you must maintain a level of humility because it is not through our giftings and abilities alone but by His grace, love and favor that we are elevated. Especially in sectors and spheres that have been typically considered to be secular, it is imperative that we maintain godly humility and allow Him to *elevate* us. Typically, when someone is the reason for your elevation, in addition to them taking the praise, those portfolios or positions can be easily revoked or rescinded. Once God has ordained and elevated you, no one can take it away from you.

Do not try to skip steps

We can rejoice, too, when we run into problems and trials, for we know that they help us develop endurance. And endurance develops strength of character, and character strengthens our confident hope of salvation. (Romans 5:3–4 NLT)

In the first chapter, when we started our conversation, we looked at Romans 5:3–5. You would agree with me that as you have journeyed through life, you would have grown. You now know things that you didn't know five years ago.

Experiences and situations equip us to better face our current circumstances. Simply put, if you had not gone through all your trials and experiences, you wouldn't have learned from them to arrive where you are today. So don't skip steps, as each step pushes you to the next. Envision yourself ascending a ladder or a flight of stairs; the probability of falling drastically increases if you try to jump a rung of the ladder or advance several steps at a time.

Take heed lest we fall

> If you think you are standing strong,
> be careful not to fall. (1 Corinthians
> 10:12 NLT)

If we do not follow God's instructions, we can be demoted. Take Saul in Samuel 15. He did not carry out the full instructions to destroy everything. God decided to remove him from the throne and make David king. Let me put it this way: don't you get irritated when people don't follow your instructions? Ouch! Sometimes we think if we follow partially, it is enough, but God requires full surrender.

We know pride goes before a fall. Sometimes pride displays itself as self-sufficiency rather than God-dependency. As I stated in the humility section, it is important to continue to give God the glory when we *elevate*. In any army or company, following strategy is critical. If you don't follow the strategic plans to a T, just one minor error or failure can derail the overall plan. You may reach higher than you were before but may not go as far as you could have gone. In order for you to move up in rank, you have to be able to follow instructions.

No half-picked ducks

Second Kings 13:14–19 tells us the final prophecy of Elisha and King Jehoash who was seeking intervention in a war with Aram. What is interesting is that Elisha was ill, but he was still doing God's work even in his last days. I encourage you to read the account, but to summarize, Elisha tells the king that the Lord has released an arrow of victory over Aram. Then Elisha instructs him to pick up the other arrows and strike the ground. Instead of repeatedly striking, the king hits the ground only three times.

There are times the Lord tells us *ARISE*, advance, go up, because He is going to *elevate* us, but instead of going all the way with full force we start the upward climb and stop. Sometimes it is the pressure of life that creates an invisible glass ceiling; at times voices from the past are shouting louder than the voice of God, which is the wind that raises you up. You do not want to be like King Jehoash, who angered the prophet because he did not go the full distance to ensure victory. The prophet said if he had continued striking, Aram would have been entirely destroyed.

The concept of a "half-picked duck" is precisely that—a bird that is being prepared for cooking but isn't cleaned well. The phrase signifies a job not completed properly. Part of being prepared to be elevated is having the mind-set that if God or a leader gives instructions, we follow them to the best of our ability, with passion and not partially.

Study to show thyself approved

> Work hard so you can present yourself to God and receive his approval. Be a good worker, one who does not need to be ashamed and who correctly explains the word of truth. (2 Timothy 2:15 NLT)

Allow me to be concise here. Some of us are prone to prepare more for the secular parts of our lives while only giving God minimal pieces of our time. We need to study to show ourselves approved unto God. In both arenas, it is important to be the best at the level where you are and, more so, prepare for advancement if the Lord decides to *elevate* you. Jesus is the perfect example, as the *word* says, He grew in wisdom and stature and favor with God and man.

CALL TO ACTION – Review the four previous calls to action, as this would be your strategy for elevation moving forward. Occasionally assess if you are reaching God's milestone for where He wants you to be, in all aspects of your life. Seek God for when He is getting ready to *ELEVATE* you and pursue Him for a new strategy.

_____

_____

_____

_____

_____

_____

_____

_____

7

A.R.I.S.E.

AS WE CLOSE THIS JOURNEY TOGETHER, LET ME LEAVE YOU with some final thoughts to reflect on as we *A.R.I.S.E.* I want to encourage those who may not have had complete success as yet in ministry, family life, or business with the following story. It is the story of the disciples fishing all night without catching anything. Sometimes you may feel like this, as though you have been stuck or have not had success for a long time. Jesus appears and directs them to throw their nets on the right side of the boat. Suddenly, their nets started to burst because of the abundance. Sometimes we are in the right area but the wrong spot. We just need to adjust in order to receive all that God has in store for us.

If we want to avoid being defeated time and time again, we cannot use the same tactics. It requires different responses.

If you feel too tired to *A.R.I.S.E.*, remember we are in a marathon, not a sprint, do not run ahead too quickly before you get burnt out. Isaiah 40:31 (AMP) states:

But those who wait for the Lord [who
expect, look for, and hope in Him]
Will gain new strength *and* renew
their power;
They will lift up their wings [and rise
up close to God] like eagles [rising
toward the sun];
They will run and not become weary,
They will walk and not grow tired.

I know at times we may doubt. Is it okay to
doubt? It happens, but we must not entertain our
doubts. When I was preparing to sit my CXC exam
(high school diploma), it was said when in doubt
choose C. I say, when in doubt choose Christ, every
time! Listen to sermons; have conversations with
God. Be reminded that His thoughts and His ways
are much higher than ours; although we may not
understand everything, He who started a good
work in us is able to complete it.

Hebrews 12:1 (NLT) says, "Therefore, since we
are surrounded by such a huge crowd of witnesses
to the life of faith, let us strip off every weight that

slows us down, especially the sin that so easily trips us up. And let us run with endurance the race God has set before us." So remove what is slowing you down, and remember there are many examples of people just like you and me whom God used in different facets of life.

God is there to help in our weakness, and He is strong. God's yoke is easy, and His burden is light. Take an analogy of the gym: you need someone to help spot you when you're trying to lift or push more weight. This is the person who's there to support you and remove the weight if it becomes too heavy.

One time when I was at the gym, I had a friend who was spotting me and encouraged me to do a heavier weight. As I was struggling to finish my set, I felt the weights became heavier. He encouraged me to finish. When I did, he told me to look around and I was left red-faced, totally embarrassed because there were no weights on the bar I was lifting. At some point during my set, he took off the weights but mentally I perceived it was heavy.

My point here is that frequently God has already taken away the burdens or weights to make things lighter but we are still in a place where we are lifting weights that are no longer there. Recognize when Jesus is dealing with a situation.

As you *A.R.I.S.E.*, I want to encourage you to:

PUSH — PRAY UNTIL SOMETHING HAPPENS

Pray without ceasing. (1 Thessalonians 5:17)

So I say to you, ask, and it will be given to you; seek, and you will find; knock, and it will be opened to you. For everyone who asks receives, and he who seeks finds, and to him who knocks it will be opened. (Luke 11:9–10)

PUSH — PRAISE UNTIL SOMETHING HAPPENS

But at midnight Paul and Silas were praying and singing hymns to God, and the prisoners were listening to them. Suddenly there was a great earthquake, so that the foundations of the prison were shaken; and immediately all the doors were opened and everyone's chains were loosed. (Acts 16:25–26 NKJV)

PUSH - PURSUE UNTIL SOMETHING HAPPENS

Seek the Lord and his strength, seek his face continually. (1 Chronicles 16:11)

Seek the Kingdom of God above all else, and live righteously, and he will give you everything you need. (Matthew 6:33 NLT)

Being your best self happens when you spend time with God and you allow Him to change you into who He wants *you* to be.

My question to you is—What is preventing you from ARISING?

So *A.R.I.S.E. – AWAKE, RESIST, INCREASE, SHINE, ELEVATE*!

ACKNOWLEDGMENTS

I want to give shout-outs to my entire family. To my wonderful wife; God has truly sent me a helpmate. He knows that I could not accomplish this without your countless "lectures," pushes, typing, support, and love.

To my son; when I set my deadlines, I love the way that you started counting down and kept letting me know if I was going to miss a deadline. At seven (7) you can be very persistent, and even though I don't like it at times, it makes you a great coach; you need those persons in your life.

To my daughter who may not be comprehending all that's happening at the age of three (3); I just love the fact that you are so caring and would give hugs and kisses when needed.

To my sisters who ensured that I would do my best always; thank you. The time you both took to review and give comments is appreciated. The frank assessments with love always pushed me.

To my parents; your endless support is treasured. I value my mother for the continuous prayers and conversations about serving Christ and my dad who would support whenever and wherever he can.

What I love most about my family is that we see past each other's faults, most days at least, but always help where we can.

Forever grateful.

Printed in the United States
by Baker & Taylor Publisher Services